THE TAKING TREE

THE TAKING TREE

by
Dan Ewen

illustrated by
Tom Richner

TERDLE Books

THE TAKING TREE
TERDLE Books
Printed in the United States of America.
ISBN 1453781773
EAN-13 9781453781777

For
Christopher
Gardner
Lauren
Madelyn
Moxie

Once there was a sweet and

naive little boy...

who
thought it
would
be nice to
plant
an apple seed.

APP

50¢
each

He liked the taste
of apples,
and thought,
"I could have my
own
apple-making
best friend.
How nifty!"
Before long, an itty bitty
sprout
pushed through
the ground.

"Hello Boy," said the sprout.

"I'm a thirsty little thing.

How about you getting me

some water?

Like

a pretty good amount of it.

Maybe

a few gallons?"

He ran off to fetch
the water. The boy
loved the baby apple tree.

And the tree knew it.

The boy collected an awful
lot of heavy water from the well,
several acres away. He toiled
to carry the many buckets of water,
finally stumbling to where the
sprout grew. The tired boy watered his
new friend.

And the tree was happy.

Every day the boy
came to water
his little
apple tree,
which...

seemed

to be

growing

bigger

by

the

hour.

"Play with me," said the boy. "How about we pretend you're my little brother?" asked the boy. "I have no siblings, which makes me feel horrible most of the time."

The baby apple tree

patted the boy

briefly

on the back,

but did not play with him.

Finally,

the boy jumped

on the tree's trunk,

and

started to climb.

The tree
quickly pushed
the boy
back to the ground.
"Whoa, easy there,
champ," said
the tree.

"Can I please
swing from your branches?
Just a little?"
asked the boy.
The tree grimaced
a bit.
"You'd better not.
I'm kinda just
getting going here."

The boy sighed, but
he was glad to see the tree
growing big and strong.
He loved the tree.

And the tree knew it.

In time, the tree began to sprout it's first apples. The boy grew taller, and his voice became a little deeper. He suddenly found himself compelled to go play with the girls in the neighborhood. But when he headed out to do so,

the tree stopped him.

"Come here Boy," said the tree.
"Check the nitrogen levels
in my soil, so I can
grow bigger and
stronger."

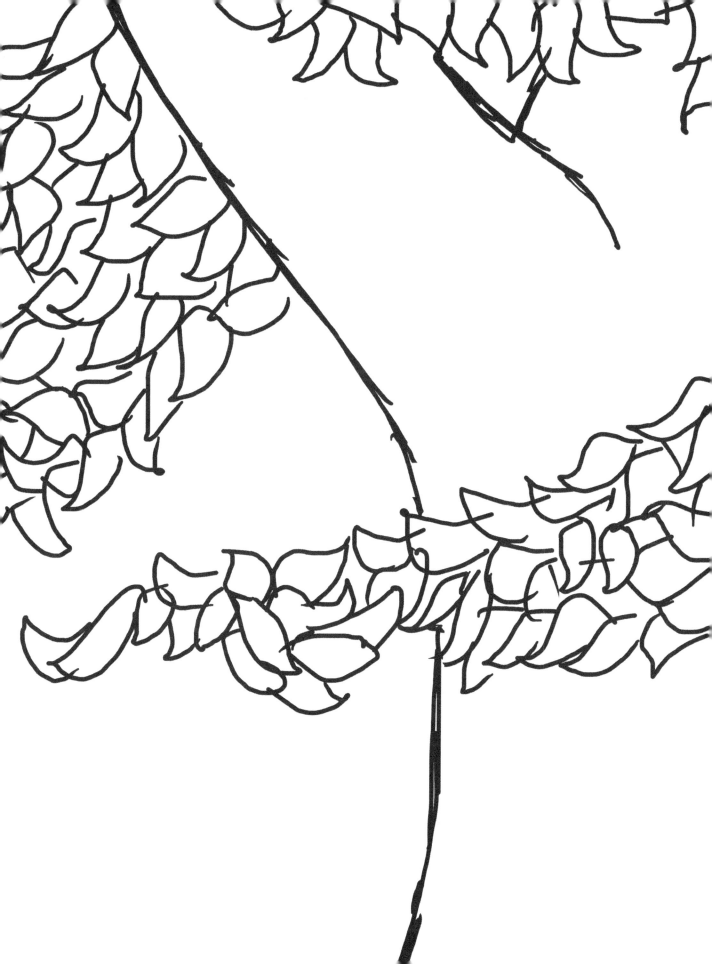

The boy explained that he didn't know how to do so. The tree sort of looked away.

"Okay. That's fine. You don't really have to, I suppose."

And so the boy felt
guilty, and learned
how to check the soil.
"While you're at it,
can you also check the
phosphorus, potassium,
magnesium, calcium
and boron?"

asked the tree,
lowering its
branches a bit to appear
especially unhealthy.

The boy sighed, and kept working as the neighborhood girls went to play elsewhere. Soon, the soil was perfect.

And
the tree
was
happy.

Before long the boy

was applying

to go to college

far away. The tree

looked on sadly as

the boy filled out

his application in

its shade.

Later, when the boy took
a nap, the tree secretly
changed his application.
The boy's entrance essay,
titled 'Why I Love Science',
was changed to
'Why I Killed a Man in
New Mexico Last Month'.
The tree also filled in
they boy's full name as
"Pooper Booger McTurdahan".

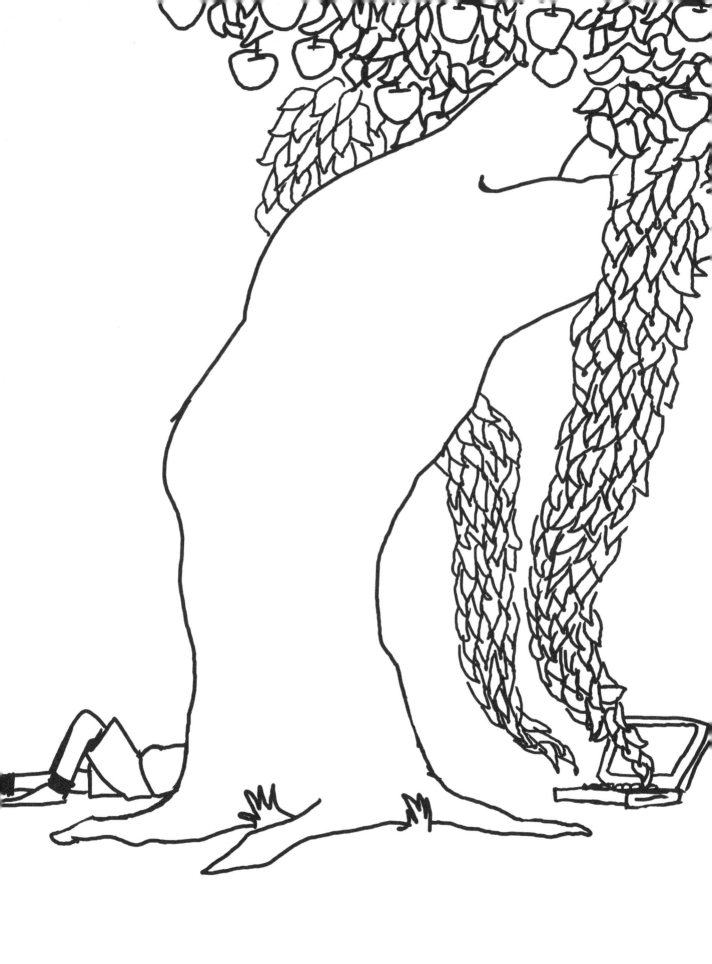

So, the boy never
heard from the college,
and instead stayed near
the tree. They would talk
for hours, although the tree did
most of the talking,
while the boy smiled
politely. The young ladies

would pass by, glancing

for a moment at

"that guy

who talks to trees",

before hurrying

away.

One day the boy
went to the tree.
"I need a house to get a
wife," said the boy. "Do you think
I could have some branches to build
one?" The tree winced. "You know,
I hear brick is much more cost
effective. Plus, a lush tree
in your yard will help
the overall property
value."

So the tree
watched as the boy
toiled day and night to build
a brick house. A few
women stopped by to admire
the house...

but when they entered
the yard the tree slung
apples at them until they
ran away.

The boy grew

lonely,

and used his computer

to arrange

for a date with

another lonely person.

But when the boy

was about to

leave,

the tree cried out.

"Boy, come quick, I've been invaded by an Eastern strain of the apple maggot! Go get some pesticide, or my fruit will be ruined."

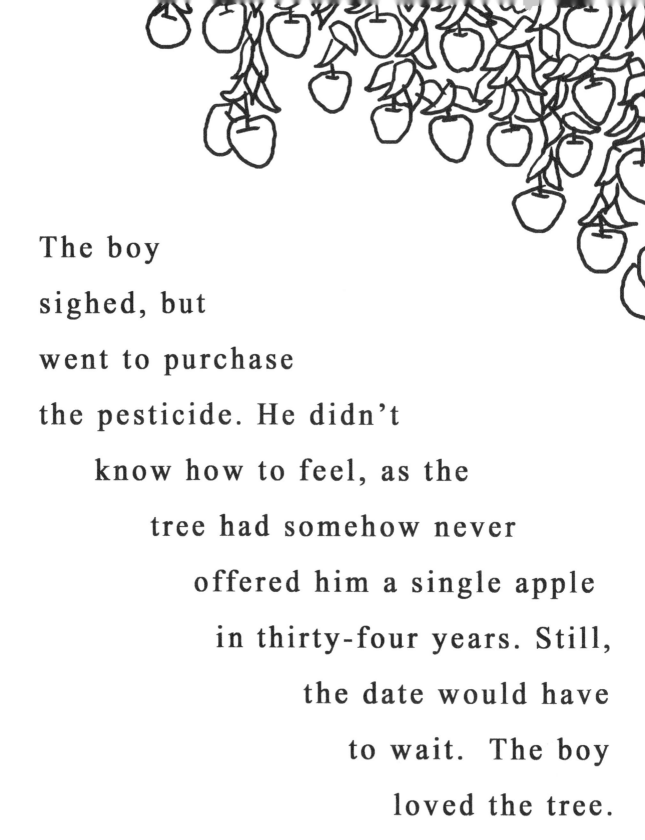

The boy
sighed, but
went to purchase
the pesticide. He didn't
know how to feel, as the
tree had somehow never
offered him a single apple
in thirty-four years. Still,
the date would have
to wait. The boy
loved the tree.

And
the
tree
knew
it.

Every time the boy tried
to meet someone new, the tree
would come calling.

"Help! Spider mites!"
"Help! Wooly aphids!"
"Help! Curculio beetles!"

The boy
spent
all of his
time
helping
the
tree.

And the
tree was
happy.

Soon, the boy's hair turned grey. Wrinkles appeared on his face, and he grew weary.

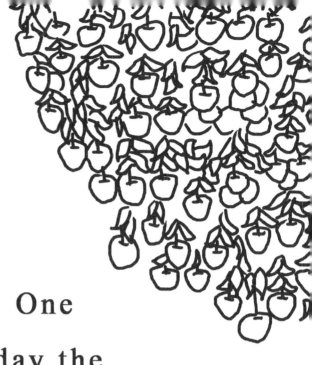

One
day the
boy limped
to the
tree and said, "My
teeth have grown weak. All
I can eat is applesauce. Can I
please have a few apples?" "Of
course," said the tree. "Climb
on up Boy, and get a few."

The boy

tried to climb the tree,

but couldn't

make it

even a

few

feet

up.

The tree giggled a bit. "Sorry
Charlie." The boy limped away,
glaring back at the tree for
the first time. That little
sprout of yesteryear
had become
a faint
memory.

Now the boy stayed inside.

After a while, the tree came

calling.

"Boy,

a

little

water?"

The boy ignored

the tree.

"Boy, there's
this great
new fertilizer
I heard
about."
The boy
did
nothing.

"Boy.
The
apple
maggots
are
back!"

But the boy refused to budge.

The tree
became angry,
and grew its
roots under the
house, through the
floorboards.
The boy
grabbed a
hatchet...

and
started
chopping
at the roots.
This only
made the tree
more angry, and soon
it smashed the roof in with
one of its mighty branches.

The tree
launched a
seemingly
endless
volley of
apples into
the house at
the boy,

who was struck in the upper neck,
lower leg, and middle armpit.

The boy managed to escape
through the front door,
staggering out
of the tree's
reach.

The angry boy limped around the neighborhood, gathering every small boy who was about to plant a seed, just like he had so many moons before. He offered them each $20, and brought them to the hardware store, equipping them with chainsaws.

Soon,
the boy
attacked
the tree with
his mercenary army.

The tree roared,
prepared for war.
Branches sliced
through
the air.
Apples
rained
like
bombs.
The
battle
raged.

Finally, the tree was almost toppled. It had launched all of its branches and apples, and was defenseless. The boy limped to what remained of the tree's trunk, revving his chainsaw. Now the tree whispered, "Boy, I love you. Allow me to whip you up some applesauce. You know, it's never too late to go to college. Perhaps I can find you a good woman?

I know some very eligble ladies. Primo gals. Barely Senior Citizens. Seriously."

The boy wiped
a trickle of
blood
from the side
of his mouth,
then splintered what
remained
of the tree's
trunk in an
instant.

It crumbled to the ground
in a lifeless heap.

The boy made his way
to the fallen tree.

Then, choking back tears...

he peed on it.

The boy made the little
boys promise never
to plant anything for the
rest of their lives.

They agreed not to,
and left to spend their
twenty dollars on the girls
in the neighborhood.

The boy headed
inside, dying moments
later in the welcoming
arms of his sagging
recliner.

And he was happy.

The End

Made in the USA
Las Vegas, NV
19 June 2024